101 Things You Should *Never* Say to Your Spouse

101 Things You Should *Never* Say to Your Spouse

Authors
Peter R. Garber
and
Nancy C. Garber

First Edition

Oshawa, Ontario

101 Things You Should Never Say to Your Spouse
By Peter R. Garber and Nancy C. Garber

Acquisitions Editor: Kevin Aguanno
Copy Editor: Josette Coppola
Typesetting: Jennifer Rumbach
Cover Design: Troy O'Brien

Published by:
Multi-Media Publications Inc.
Box 58043, Rosslynn RPO, Oshawa, Ontario, Canada, L1J 8L6

http://www.mmpubs.com/

All rights reserved. No part of this book may be reproduced or transmitted in any form or by any means, electronic or mechanical, including photocopying, recording or by any information storage and retrieval system, without written permission from the author, except for the inclusion of brief quotations in a review.

Copyright © 2007 by Peter R. Garber and Nancy C. Garber

Paperback: (ISBN-10) 1-897326-00-9
Adobe PDF eBook: (ISBN-10) 1-897326-01-7
Microsoft LIT eBook: (ISBN-10) 1-897326-02-5
Mobipocket PRC eBook: (ISBN-10) 1-897326-03-3
Palm PDB eBook: (ISBN-10) 1-897326-04-1

Published in Canada. Printed simultaneously in the U.S.A. and in England.

Table of Contents

Foreword 13
Introduction 19

Feelings 23
1. "YOU KNOW HOW I FEEL ABOUT YOU."
2. "I'M NOT SORRY."
3. "I DON'T WANT TO SAY ANYTHING BAD ABOUT YOU, BUT . . . ."
4. "I CAN'T FORGIVE YOU FOR THIS."
5. "YOU'RE MORE INTERESTED IN YOUR HOBBY THAN IN ME."
6. "YOU SHOULDN'T FEEL THAT WAY."
7. "I JUST SAID THAT TO HURT YOU."

Perceptions 29
8. "YOU'RE WRONG AGAIN."
9. "I DON'T LIKE THE WAY YOU DRIVE."
10. "I DON'T LIKE THAT ON YOU."
11. "I DON'T THINK YOU WERE RIGHT."
12. "YOU'RE SUCH A BIG BABY WHEN YOU ARE SICK."
13. "YOU WILL JUST HAVE TO FORGIVE ME FOR THIS."

14. "IF YOU WANT MY OPINION . . . ."
15. "WHY CAN'T YOU BE MORE LIKE SO-AND-SO?"
16. "DON'T WEAR THAT."
17. "I DON'T KNOW WHY YOU DISLIKE SO-AND-SO."
18. "I DON'T WANT TO COMPLAIN, BUT . . ."
19. "I THINK HE OR SHE IS SOOOOO GOOD-LOOKING."
20. "WHY CAN'T YOU BE MORE ___?"
21. "YOU HAVE NO SENSE OF HUMOR."

Tastes 41

22. "WE ALWAYS DO WHAT YOU WANT TO DO."
23. "LET'S TALK ABOUT WHAT I WANT TO TALK ABOUT."
24. "I'll PICK OUT WHAT DVD WE WATCH."
25. "YOU KNOW HOW MUCH I HATE THAT."
26. "THIS WILL LOOK GREAT ON YOU."
27. "I'M WEARING IT ANYWAY."
28. "WHY DID YOU BUY THAT?"
29. "I KNOW THIS IS A PET PEEVE OF YOURS."
30. "DO WE HAVE TO SEE YOUR FAMILY SO SOON AGAIN?"
31. "I'M SICK OF HEARING ABOUT YOUR HOBBY."

32. "I'LL DECIDE WHAT CAR WE BUY."
33. "I'LL MAKE ALL OUR DECORATING DECISIONS."
34. "I LIKED YOUR HAIR BETTER BEFORE YOU GOT IT CUT."
35. "YOU LOOK FAT IN THAT."

Communication 51

36. "I CAN'T TELL YOU."
37. "DID I TELL YOU WHAT I DID TO THE CAR?"
38. "I FORGOT TO GIVE YOU A PHONE MESSAGE."
39. "I'M NOT GOING TO LISTEN TO YOU."
40. "I DON'T WANT TO TALK ABOUT IT."
41. "YOU KNOW WHAT I MEANT."
42. "I DIDN'T THINK YOU WOULD MIND IF I TOLD PEOPLE ABOUT YOUR ____"
43. "WHAT ARE YOU THINKING ABOUT?"
44. "I KNOW HOW MUCH YOU HATE TO HEAR THIS."
45. "YEAH, I'M LISTENING."
46. "I'M NOT LISTENING TO YOU ANYMORE."
47. "I DIDN'T KNOW YOU WANTED ME TO CALL."
48. "I THOUGHT I TOLD YOU I WAS GOING TO BE LATE."

Schedules 61
49. "I DON'T HAVE TIME TO TALK ABOUT IT."
50. "I'LL SEND YOU AN E-MAIL INSTEAD OF CALLING."
51. "I'M TOO BUSY TO MEET YOU FOR LUNCH."
52. "I CAN NEVER SEEM TO REMEMBER WHEN WE ARE SUPPOSED TO DO THINGS TOGETHER."
53. "I CHANGED OUR PLANS."

Time Off 67
54. "YOU'VE GOT TO READ THIS BOOK."
55. "I NEED MORE TIME TO MYSELF."
56. "I'LL DECIDE WHERE WE GO ON VACATION."
57. "I DON'T WANT TO DO ANYTHING NEW OR DIFFERENT TOGETHER."
58. "GIVE ME THE TV CLICKER."
59. "I DON'T FEEL LIKE GOING AWAY TOGETHER THIS WEEKEND."
60. "LET'S EAT AT HOME AGAIN TONIGHT."
61. "LET'S NOT DO ANYTHING SPECIAL THIS HOLIDAY."
62. "LET ME READ THE SUNDAY PAPER FIRST."
63. "GIVE ME A BACK MASSAGE."

64. "DO WE HAVE TO GO OUT WITH THEM?"
65. "JUST READ MY MAGAZINES INSTEAD OF SUBSCRIBING TO YOUR OWN."
66. "I'LL CHOOSE THE MOVIE WE SEE TONIGHT."

Roles 79

67. "YOU DO ALL THE COOKING."
68. "YOU MAKE THE COFFEE IN THE MORNING."
69. "I'M SICK OF HEARING ABOUT YOUR WORK."
70. "DON'T WORRY ABOUT YOUR JOB SO MUCH."
71. "TAKE OUT THE GARBAGE."

Compatibility 85

72. "I'M NOT GOING TO FIGHT FAIR."
73. "I WON'T LET IT GO."
74. "I DON'T FEEL LIKE TAKING A WALK TOGETHER."
75. "YOU ARE SO PREDICTABLE."
76. "YOU'RE ALWAYS IN A BAD MOOD."
77. "WHAT'S BUGGING YOU?"
78. "IS THAT SMELL YOU?"
79. "YOU SHOULD HAVE KNOWN THAT I NEEDED HELP."
80. "YOU'LL NEVER CHANGE MY MIND."

Lifestyles 93

81. "WHY SHOULD WE WORRY ABOUT RETIREMENT PLANNING NOW?"
82. "I WAS GOING TO BUY IT FOR YOU BUT IT WAS TOO EXPENSIVE."
83. "WHY DID YOU THROW THAT OUT?"
84. "WHAT'S FOR BREAKFAST?"
85. "STOP PUTTING IT OFF AND JUST DO IT."
86. "I FORGOT TO TELL YOU WHAT I BOUGHT."
87. "I DIDN'T KNOW YOU WANTED TO GO."

Romance 101

88. "WHO CARES ABOUT REMINISCING ABOUT WHEN WE FIRST MET?"
89. "WE'RE MARRIED, SO WE CAN'T GO ON DATES ANYMORE."
90. "IT'S STUPID TO CELEBRATE OUR ANNIVERSARY."
91. "DON'T CALL ME THAT ANYMORE."
92. "I DIDN'T HAVE TIME TO GET YOU A CARD."
93. "I DON'T NEED TO SAY 'THANK YOU' TO YOU."
94. "I'M NOT GOING TO WEAR MY WEDDING RING ANYMORE."

95. "WHY DO YOU WANT TO HOLD HANDS?"
96. "I DON'T LIKE TO KISS ANYMORE."
97. "I FORGOT TO BUY YOU A PRESENT."
98. "SURE, I MISSED YOU WHEN YOU WERE GONE."
99. "I DON'T WANT TO TALK ABOUT US."
100. "I DON'T HAVE TO WORRY ABOUT MY APPEARANCE ANYMORE—YOU'LL LOVE ME ANYWAY."
101. "I DON'T FEEL LIKE MAKING LOVE."

About the Authors 111

Foreword

When you've been married for any period of time, there are of course going to be things you say to your spouse that probably shouldn't be said at all. This book is filled with many of the statements that married people make to one another that aren't always very well received. Saying these types of things to your partner is part of being married, and a marriage must be able to survive these comments if it is going to survive at all.

However, the immediate result of these remarks may vary greatly with each marriage. Couples may learn to be patient and understanding about these "slips of the tongue," choosing to turn the other cheek in order to keep peace in the family. On the other hand, these statements may cause husbands or wives to become angry at one another, perhaps even triggering arguments between them. Regardless, learning to be more aware of what you say and more sensitive to your spouse's feelings can only serve to strengthen your marriage.

Our own thirty-year marriage has been the research for this book. After all these years of marriage, we believe we have said almost all of these 101 things to one another in one way or another. On some occasions we have made these remarks purposely, but in other instances we have inadvertently blurted them out. Your marriage will also face many different challenges, and it can be beneficial to identify potentially problematic things you might find yourself saying to one another during these trying times.

Sometimes these comments are taken in stride with few or no repercussions, and at other times they hit a more sensitive nerve. Like most couples, we have learned precisely which subjects each of us considers "off limits" and which ones might be more open to a spousal critique. Understanding this distinction is important when deciding what things you should and shouldn't ever say to your spouse. We believe that this book can help other couples learn to become more perceptive about these different levels of tolerance for various remarks.

One key element in gaining this insight is an appreciation of the differences between you and your spouse. They say that opposites attract, especially in marriage. It is perhaps this polarity that not only makes a marriage work but also makes for some interesting discussions resulting in many of these 101 things being spoken. Our marriage is certainly one punctuated by differences between us in just about everything. One of us is outgoing, and the other is reserved. One of us is cautious, while the other is a risk-taker. One of us is frugal (okay, cheap), and the other is a spendthrift. This list could go on and on.

Perhaps an analysis of the contrasts between you and your spouse would yield a similar result. If so, this book will help you better understand how to deal with your many differences in a more positive and productive manner. It will do this by preparing you for those times when you suddenly hear one of the *101 Things You Should Never Say to Your Spouse* coming from your partner's lips. Even if you and your spouse are more alike than most couples, you probably still have trouble differentiating between the things your partner may want to hear and the ones that may be far less welcome. Whatever the level of similarity is between you and your spouse, this book will help you recognize likely sources of trouble in common marital statements.

Many of these 101 remarks do not represent the major concerns that you face in your life together but rather the relatively minor ones. It's funny, though, how these seemingly trivial matters can sometimes develop into the biggest issues in a marriage. Take driving, for instance. It's not that either of us is a particularly bad driver. It is just that we tend to travel from one place to another differently.

One of us definitely gets to places much faster than the other. And although one of us wouldn't stop for directions no matter how hopelessly lost we might be (guess which one of us this is), the other would likely ask everyone and anyone encountered along the way for guidance. These differences in driving styles may seem insignificant, but they can often steer a marriage onto some very bumpy roads.

There are numerous other areas of daily life that can be potential relationship hazards. For example, one of us is late for nearly every occasion, while the other is ready hours beforehand. Even the most minor physical ailment is a major calamity for one of us, whereas the other never complains when feeling poorly. And although one is a hopeless romantic, the other almost never expresses a romantic feeling. And so it goes, the eternal yin and yang of marriage. These differences have contributed greatly to this collection of things that you shouldn't say to your spouse.

Recognizing this diversity of possible sore subjects, we have included a wide variety of topics that cover many aspects of your life together as a couple. This book is presented in ten parts: Feelings, Perceptions, Tastes, Communications, Schedules, Time Off, Roles, Compatibility, Lifestyles, and Romance. Depending upon whatever is currently going on in your lives, you and your spouse may find it helpful to focus specifically on one of these sections of the book, concentrating on the topics found there before tackling other issues.

Foreword

As you read this book, try to be more forgiving of your spouse if he or she says many of these 101 things. Take comfort, as we do, in knowing that you are not alone when it comes to being frustrated by the words that pass between husbands and wives in a marriage. The way we see it, at least we're communicating with one another. It would be much worse not to say anything to each other at all, as the success of every relationship depends on an open exchange of communications.

The more positive feedback we can give our spouses about these communications, the better our relationships will become. The problem lies not so much in saying these things to your spouse but in failing to understand how these comments might be received. Remember that as long as there is love between you and your spouse, as there is between the two of us, words can always be forgiven. You sometimes just need to find it in your heart to forgive the one you love for these things that are said.

Peter and Nancy Garber

101 Things You Should Never Say to Your Spouse

Introduction

Do you feel that you are always saying the wrong thing at the worst time to your spouse? Does it seem that the harder you try to make things better, the deeper in trouble you get? If so, do not feel that you are alone. These frustrations are shared by virtually everyone who has ever been in a romantic relationship.

Actually, this book could have been written by anyone who has been married for any period of time. Each of us has said many of these or similar things to our spouse at one time or another. By giving more thought to what we say to our partners and how he or she may react, we can avoid many of the communication problems we experience in our relationships.

101 Things You Should Never Say to Your Spouse targets these communication misfires by providing you with examples of remarks that may be needlessly upsetting your wife or husband. As in most aspects of life, we tend to make the same mistakes over and over again in all our relationships, and this is certainly true when it comes to the things we say to our spouses. We continually make the same irritating observations to our spouses that keep creating problems in our marriages. Part of breaking this cycle is not only learning what not to say but also preventing these same bad habits from resurfacing in the future. An important factor in this preventive approach is the respect you have for your mate. Most of the *101 Things You Should Never Say to Your Spouse* pertain to common courtesies that we sometimes forget to extend to our partners. Why shouldn't we show our loved ones the same consideration we offer other people in our lives?

In addition to recognizing this need for mutual regard, spouses must also reconcile attitudes that are often at odds with one another. You may find that many of these *101 Things You Should Never Say to Your Spouse* appear to be contradictory to your most natural instincts. However, marriage itself has many inconsistencies. By their very nature, husbands and wives are contradictions of each other. What one partner likes may not appeal to the other at all. To complicate matters even more, there is a situational factor at work in any exchange between husbands and wives. Everything that we say to our spouses must be considered in the context in which it is said. Some things may be acceptable in certain circumstances but may not be received well at all in others. What may appear to be contradictory may be more a function of the conditions under which it is said.

With so many of these potential obstacles, you and your spouse may need to work together to find better ways of communicating with one another. Learn which of these 101 things particularly bother your spouse. Take turns pointing out to each other the most annoying remarks and perhaps even adding ones of your own. The better you understand these hot-button issues affecting one another, the closer your relationship can become.

To simplify this process, each of these *101 Things You Should Never Say to Your Spouse* addresses a specific category of comments that husbands and wives typically make to one another. You will find that there is a better way of communicating each of these statements. Like the proverbial silver lining in every cloud, there is a positive aspect to virtually all 101 of these things. *101 Things You Should Never Say to Your Spouse* will help you by offering better methods for expressing each of these sentiments to your partner. Try them and see what a difference it can make in your relationship with your spouse. This book may serve as the best marriage counseling you will ever experience!

101 Things You Should Never Say to Your Spouse

CHAPTER ONE

Feelings

101 Things You Should Never Say to Your Spouse

1. "YOU KNOW HOW I FEEL ABOUT YOU."

Your spouse may indeed know how you feel about him or her, but that's not really the point. Your partner still needs to hear you express your feelings and affection from time to time. You can't say, "I love you" too often to your loved one. Don't keep your mate guessing about your feelings or assume that you no longer need to tell him or her how you feel. Give your spouse frequent reassurance about your love.

2. "I'M NOT SORRY."

Remember that famous line from the movie *Love Story*, "Love is never having to say you're sorry"? Well, in real life this is not necessarily true. You need to admit to your spouse when you are wrong and ask for his or her forgiveness. Many problems that couples experience can be made infinitely better by these two little words that can mean so much when you're hearing your spouse say them.

Swallow your pride and apologize to your spouse for whatever you did that may be upsetting him or her. You might find that admitting you were wrong is not so difficult to do once you get some practice. It may even provide some unexpected benefits. You might even find yourself apologizing for things that you never even did!

3. "I DON'T WANT TO SAY ANYTHING BAD ABOUT YOU, BUT . . . ."

When most people say this, they don't really mean it. If you really don't want to say anything negative, then simply *don't* say anything negative.

You probably know better than anyone what negative things you can say to your spouse that will upset him or her the most. Don't use this knowledge just to upset your partner. Save both of you the anger and frustration that often accompanies these negative remarks and keep them to yourself. Say something positive instead.

4. "I CAN'T FORGIVE YOU FOR THIS."

What ever happened to the old adage, "Forgive and forget"? Don't you think it is about time to forget what has already been said and done, whatever it was?

If you really must play the injured party every time you feel you have been wronged, then put some time limits on how long you will wait to forgive your spouse. For instance, some things may only require withholding forgiveness for a relatively short period of time, such as a few hours or even a day. Other things may take longer. The point is that you have to find it in your heart to forgive your spouse. It should be just a matter of time—and the shorter that is, the better.

5. "YOU'RE MORE INTERESTED IN YOUR HOBBY THAN IN ME."

This is a theory that you may not really want to prove. You might not like the answer you find! Of course this isn't really true. Your spouse's hobby cannot provide him or her with comfort, support, or love and wouldn't be any fun to cuddle up to at night. Then why does it seem that your spouse is sometimes more interested in his or her hobby than in you?

The best advice is to avoid trying to compete with your spouse's hobby, because you will probably lose. Hobbies are important to us as a way to unwind and relax. Our hobbies are those things that we really want to do, as opposed to all the other things in our lives that we have to do. Instead of being jealous of these activities, give your spouse the time he or she wants to pursue a hobby. Come to an agreement about when your mate will pursue his or her hobby interests. Your spouse, and ultimately you as well, will be happier as a result.

6. "YOU SHOULDN'T FEEL THAT WAY."

Why is it that you think that you can tell your spouse how he or she should feel? No one can really dictate to others what kind of emotions they are to experience. You might point out ways they are expected to feel and ultimately behave, but you cannot really change people's feelings, particularly if they are not interested in changing them.

Let your spouse feel any way he or she wants to feel and don't even try to change these emotions. You'll just be wasting your time and frustrating both of you.

7. "I JUST SAID THAT TO HURT YOU."

Like the song says, "You always hurt the one you love." Spouses sometimes say things just to hurt each other. They really don't mean all those nasty things they say to one another. They are intended only to upset their mates.

Spouses can sometimes become very skilled at saying these kinds of hurtful things to one another, but pick another aspect of your marital role to increase your expertise. Try not to say things you really don't mean simply to hurt your spouse. You'll find that you will ultimately get a lot further saying what you really mean rather than what you don't.

CHAPTER TWO

Perceptions

101 Things You Should Never Say to Your Spouse

8. "YOU'RE WRONG AGAIN."

Even if you are right, don't rub it in your spouse's face. Simply being right isn't always enough when dealing with your loved one. It is more important that you be right in a supportive way that doesn't hurt your partner's feelings. Don't make being right or wrong a win-lose situation. Find ways to share being right with your partner. Your spouse may receive comments such as "You made me think of it" or "Thanks for reminding me" much more positively than, "As usual, you are wrong again."

Find ways to work together towards solving the problems you face as a couple. Marriage is not supposed to be an "I'm right, you're wrong" competition.

9. "I DON'T LIKE THE WAY YOU DRIVE."

Criticizing the way your spouse drives seems to be part of every couple's travel plans. What is it about your partner's driving that you don't like? Does he or she drive too fast or too slow, take the longest route each time, or refuse to ever ask for directions as you drive around in circles trying to find your destination?

Whatever the case, pointing out your spouse's driving deficiencies will probably only make them worse. Try something different. Say nice things about your spouse's driving for a change (oh yes, you can), but be careful about when you do this. You don't want to shock your spouse while he or she is behind the wheel.

10. "I DON'T LIKE THAT ON YOU."

Any encounter involving the above statement is doomed to end badly. How you think something looks on your spouse is really not as important as how he or she feels about it. Make sure you know how much your spouse likes the way the item of clothing looks before you offer your critique.

This is not to say that you should never offer an honest opinion when asked by your spouse about his or her wardrobe. There are times when your partner really does want your candid thoughts on how something looks on him or her. However, even during these moments it may still be a good idea to first ask, "I don't know, how do you like it?"

11. "I DON'T THINK YOU WERE RIGHT."

Anyone who has ever been married has surely said this to his or her spouse at one time or another and has just as surely come to regret it. This statement can result in any number of different repercussions from your spouse, depending on the situation. However, you need to be sensitive to those circumstances when your spouse really needs your support regardless of your feelings of right or wrong.

During these important moments in your relationship, how you feel about what your spouse said or did may be far less important than offering encouragement when he or she needs you the most. Unconditional support is one of the most important ingredients in a successful marriage. We all need this support and affirmation from our spouses, particularly when we are upset or feeling bad about something we did or said.

12. "YOU'RE SUCH A BIG BABY WHEN YOU ARE SICK."

We all need a little tender loving care when we are not feeling well. It is also nice to receive this understanding and special treatment from your spouse. Remember that part of your wedding vows that said something about "in sickness and in health"?

Even if your spouse is a "big baby" about being sick, you still need to take special care of him or her. Also, don't mention the fact that he or she acts this way when sick, at least not too often. It may only make the symptoms worse and the recovery time longer.

13. "YOU WILL JUST HAVE TO FORGIVE ME FOR THIS."

This is a good example of wishful thinking. Just saying this doesn't mean that it is going to happen. Wouldn't it be nice if this approach did work? You could have your spouse's forgiveness for just about anything you do by repeating those nine magic words, "You will just have to forgive me for this!"

Your spouse's forgiveness is not something you can simply wish for or assume to be automatically yours for the taking at all times. In some circumstances, your spouse's forgiveness may be something you must earn. You should have to work hard for it and never take it for granted.

14. "IF YOU WANT MY OPINION . . . ."

The truth of the matter is that there are times when your spouse's answer to this statement is "no." He or she may not want or appreciate your opinion at all. To help you better understand when your spouse might want your opinion and when he or she may not, use the following rule as a guide: If you find yourself saying, "If you want my opinion . . . ," then it is probably not wanted.

If your spouse really wants your opinion, he or she will most likely ask you for it. Offering your opinion at other times will undoubtedly set you up to hear something that sounds like, "If I want your opinion, I'll ask for it!"

15. "WHY CAN'T YOU BE MORE LIKE SO-AND-SO?"

Most people have said this to their spouses in one way or another at some time in their marriage. Despite the phrase's popularity, there is probably no other more universally disliked and unappreciated statement that you could make to your spouse.

Your spouse can't be more like So-and-So. What's more, you should be glad that your spouse is not like So-and-So. Did it ever occur to you that So-and-So's spouse might be asking him or her to be more like your spouse? Wouldn't that be ironic?

16. "DON'T WEAR THAT."

Being married can mean that you no longer have control of your wardrobe. Every clothing purchase may now be subject to the scrutiny and approval of your spouse. Even after an item of apparel has passed these initial tests, it still needs to be reviewed by your mate to judge its appropriateness for the occasion.

You need to be careful as to how often and in what circumstances you choose to exercise your "spousal wardrobe approval rights." You should try to ensure that your partner accepts your clothing feedback as much as possible. This may mean that there will be times when it is best to keep your opinions to yourself and let your spouse feel comfortable with what he or she has selected to wear, even if it does look truly awful.

17. "I DON'T KNOW WHY YOU DISLIKE SO-AND-SO."

You already know that your spouse doesn't like this person. In fact, it is likely that your mate has made this fact very clear to you on numerous occasions. What do you think are the chances that you will be able to change how your spouse feels about this particular individual?

Although this is not always the case, there is usually some expectation between partners in a marriage that they will both dislike the same people. This makes it much easier to talk about these people, and both spouses gain a certain sense of satisfaction in expressing this shared distain for these individuals. However, if you and your mate are of differing opinions about someone, it can be much more uncomfortable to talk about this person. In this case, it is probably best not to even mention this individual's name, much less try to change your spouse's opinion of him or her.

18. "I DON'T WANT TO COMPLAIN, BUT . . ."

In reality most of us like to complain, particularly to our spouses. And we like to complain not only *to* our spouses but also *about* our spouses. Saying to your partner, "I don't want to complain about you" is probably not quite true. If you are married, you probably love to complain about your mate.

The only people who really benefit from griping about their spouses are comedians who make their livings by complaining about their partners' peculiarities. Unless you are going to develop your marital woes into a nightclub act and become a famous comic, try to keep your grumbling about your spouse to a minimum. You'll have a lot more laughs at home as a result.

19. "I THINK HE OR SHE IS SOOOOO GOOD-LOOKING."

Even if you do think that someone other than your spouse is extremely good-looking, it might be better for your marriage if you kept your opinion to yourself. Although it may be permissible to make an occasional comment about someone of the opposite sex, you shouldn't go overboard in your appraisal. It is likely that your spouse may not share your enthusiasm about how handsome or beautiful you think the other person is.

A statement such as, "I think he or she is sooooo good-looking" probably doesn't make your spouse feel more secure about his or her own looks. Why not say something nice about your partner's appearance instead? You can be sure that it will be better received.

20. "WHY CAN'T YOU BE MORE ___?"

This is one in which you can fill in the blank space yourself with any number of characteristics that you may wish your spouse possessed. You might say something like, "Why can't you be more sensitive?" or "Why can't you be more romantic?" or ask for anything else that you could ever desire in a spouse. But wishing for something and having it become a reality are two different things. You probably will only upset your spouse by saying these things, and expressing these kinds of wishes will not make them come true anyway. Don't wish for what you may not be able to have and instead be happy with all the good things you already like about your spouse.

21. "YOU HAVE NO SENSE OF HUMOR."

"Come on, can't you take a joke?"

"Don't you have a sense of humor anymore?"

"Lighten up a little bit."

"Don't take life so seriously."

Do any of these remarks ever really make you laugh or even smile when your spouse says them to you? If not, why do you think these or similar expressions will have a humorous effect on your spouse?

Maybe the reason you think that your spouse doesn't have a sense of humor is simply that he or she doesn't agree with you about what is funny. Did it ever occur to you that your spouse might think that you are the one who's missing a funny bone? Lighten up a little on the remarks about your spouse's sense of humor.

101 Things You Should Never Say to Your Spouse

CHAPTER THREE

Tastes

101 Things You Should Never Say to Your Spouse

22. "WE ALWAYS DO WHAT YOU WANT TO DO."

Does it seem that as a couple you two always do what your spouse wants to do? Is this really true or is it just the way it seems to you? Saying this to your spouse will undoubtedly cause him or her to disagree. Be prepared to hear a list of things that you did together that you supposedly wanted to do. Remember, spouses sometimes have long memories for these kinds of things. How long is your memory?

23. "LET'S TALK ABOUT WHAT I WANT TO TALK ABOUT."

These are probably not the best words you could choose to begin a conversation with your spouse. Husbands and wives often have very different things they like to talk about most. Each must give the other a turn in choosing what they discuss. Always trying to lead the conversation toward what you want to talk about can really become boring for your spouse. Give equal time to your mate or be prepared to lose some of his or her interest in talking to you.

24. "I'll PICK OUT WHAT DVD WE WATCH."

You may consider yourself the world's greatest authority on what DVD movie to watch at home this weekend. However, your spouse may want to challenge your credentials.

Let your partner have a say concerning which movies to rent the next time you go to the video store or use an online service. Remember that you are not the only one who will watch the movie. You may even enjoy your spouse's choices better than the ones you had in mind.

25. "YOU KNOW HOW MUCH I HATE THAT."

Surely your spouse already has a very good idea of your likes and dislikes. There is probably no need to remind him or her of these things. Or maybe you expect your spouse to grab a pencil and paper and say, "Just in case I may have missed a few things you don't like, let me make a complete list of everything for future reference"!

26. "THIS WILL LOOK GREAT ON YOU."

Maybe you should pick out all of your spouse's clothes. After all, you know what looks best on your partner, right? You are the one who has to look at him or her. You could even take this a step further and buy all your spouse's clothes. That way anything he or she wears will always meet with your approval.

Whenever you are going out, tell your spouse what he or she should wear. If your partner tries to select his or her own clothes, just say something like, "I know what looks best on you. You'll look great in this." If your spouse ignores your advice, just say, "That doesn't look good on you" regardless of what he or she puts on. This will definitely do wonders for your mate's confidence.

Now imagine your spouse saying these things to you concerning your wardrobe. If your partner doesn't pick out your clothes, then why would you feel that you should pick out all of his or her clothes?

27. "I'M WEARING IT ANYWAY."

There are many times when you might find yourself saying this to your spouse. For instance, as you are getting ready to go out together you might say, "I know you don't like this, but I'm wearing it anyway." Or if you kept an expensive item of clothing that you promised to return, you might hear yourself saying, "I know we can't afford this, but I'm wearing it anyway" or "I don't care how it looks, I'm wearing it anyway." Okay, go ahead and wear it, but do it at your own risk.

28. "WHY DID YOU BUY THAT?"

Do you second-guess every purchase your spouse makes? Do you try to make your spouse feel guilty every time he or she brings home something new? Do you question the price and need for every purchase?

If so, you probably often say, "Why did you buy that?" to your spouse. Loosen up the purse strings just a bit. Let your spouse enjoy his or her next purchase without having to justify the expenditure or feel guilty.

29. "I KNOW THIS IS A PET PEEVE OF YOURS."

This statement is invariably followed by the word "but" and then whatever it is that bothers your spouse the most. You are probably very aware of your partner's pet peeves. If you know what these irritants are, then why do you continue to bother your spouse when you should do everything possible not to annoy him or her with whatever it is? Otherwise, you are probably only creating a new pet peeve for your mate.

30. "DO WE HAVE TO SEE YOUR FAMILY SO SOON AGAIN?"

You may indeed be thinking this. You may believe that you have already had enough personal contact recently with your in-laws to last you for quite a while. It is also possible that you may not enjoy seeing your spouse's family at all. Even if all this is true, you should never ask, "Do we have to see *your family* so soon again?"

Notice which words have been italicized above. Don't forget that there is a flip side to this issue. It is called your spouse's in-laws, or in other words YOUR FAMILY. Remember that what goes around comes around, both in life and in marriage. Your spouse may feel the same about your family as you do about his or hers.

31. "I'M SICK OF HEARING ABOUT YOUR HOBBY."

People love to talk about their hobbies, generally because these activities are what interests them the most. Unfortunately, your spouse's hobby may not be of any interest to you. However, you need to allow your spouse some time to tell you about his or her pursuit of this hobby. In turn, you should also have equal time to talk about your hobby and interests. Learn what you can about each other's hobbies and maybe you will even become eager to hear more about your spouse's interests.

32. "I'LL DECIDE WHAT CAR WE BUY."

Other than buying your home, the purchase of a car is probably the largest expenditure you will ever make in your life together. Particularly with the high cost of buying a car today, this purchase is a major investment. Because of this expense, people tend to keep their cars longer than ever before. Car owners today may drive their vehicles for even seven to ten years or more to get the most mileage from their purchases.

Don't you think something this important that will be part of your lives for most of the next decade deserves at least to be discussed with your partner?

33. "I'LL MAKE ALL OUR DECORATING DECISIONS."

It is unlikely that you and your spouse have exactly the same tastes in decorating. Regardless of how interested you or your spouse might be in interior design, it is still something you have to look at every minute you spend at home.

You and your spouse should make joint decisions about how to decorate your home. After all, you both live there.

34. "I LIKED YOUR HAIR BETTER BEFORE YOU GOT IT CUT."

The best time to say this is definitely not immediately after your spouse gets his or her hair cut. By then, the time to have expressed this deep attachment to the former hairstyle has already passed. Now it's too late to do anything about it. Once hair is cut, all you can do is learn to live with it until it grows back.

What good does it do anyone to make disparaging remarks about your spouse's recent haircut after the fact? The best thing to do at this point is simply to say how nice you think it looks and then silently wait for it to grow.

35. "YOU LOOK FAT IN THAT."

These words have preceded some of the worst experiences in marital history. It doesn't matter if it is true or not; it still shouldn't be said. Saying, "You look fat in that" will only cause you to regret ever having spoken these words. You will probably spend the next hour or more trying to explain that you really didn't mean to say that your spouse appears a bit heavier in those clothes. There are many other things that you might say about your mate's appearance in a new outfit or about a wardrobe choice for an outing. Think of something, in fact anything, other than, "You look fat in that." Your spouse will feel a lot thinner as a result.

CHAPTER FOUR

Communication

101 Things You Should Never Say to Your Spouse

36. "I CAN'T TELL YOU."

"I can't tell you" might be an acceptable response if you were working on a top-secret government project whose discovery could compromise our nation's security, but it probably won't be very well received by your spouse. Husbands and wives really should not have any secrets between them. You need to be able to share even the most personal information with each other. This of course comes with the responsibility to do nothing to jeopardize this trust. And yes, this means not using this information against each other when angry or engaged in a fight.

37. "DID I TELL YOU WHAT I DID TO THE CAR?"

This question could be followed by any number of different things. For instance, you could go on to tell your spouse that you washed and waxed the car, that you paid off the remainder of the car loan, or that you had the oil and filter changed today.

On the other hand, you might go on to explain something less positive, such as a scratch, dent, or major damage that the car just acquired. Unfortunately, it seems that most news about a car following this question is not good. Break this kind of news about the car to your spouse gently and at a time when he or she may be able to accept it without too much weeping.

38. "I FORGOT TO GIVE YOU A PHONE MESSAGE."

People often mistakenly think that if they give a message to someone to pass on to a spouse, it will be successfully delivered. Unfortunately, this is not always (or usually) the case. How many times do you end up saying to your spouse, "Oh, I guess I must have forgotten to give you that message"? This is usually only discovered after your spouse has experienced either embarrassment and/or major difficulties due to your poor communications.

Make sure that you relay all the messages you are asked to deliver to your spouse. If you don't, you might find your spouse's memory failing as well when it comes to remembering to give you your messages.

39. "I'M NOT GOING TO LISTEN TO YOU."

In other words, you're going to do whatever you darn well please! Why should you bother listening to your spouse?

After all, your spouse is only the one who serves as your partner in life, knows you better than anyone else in this world, and has a vested interest in every aspect of you!

You need to listen to what your spouse has to say and at least carefully consider his or her opinions. You might not always agree with your partner, but you do need to understand his or her views.

40. "I DON'T WANT TO TALK ABOUT IT."

This will certainly quickly end any conversation that you may be having with your spouse. It will also make your spouse very upset. But perhaps that was your objective in stating that you didn't want to talk about it in the first place?

Shutting down communications with your spouse probably will do nothing but worsen whatever misunderstanding you two may be having. You need to be willing to openly discuss anything with your mate. This is the only way you can realistically expect your spouse to understand how you feel about the subject you are refusing to talk about.

41. "YOU KNOW WHAT I MEANT."

Sometimes we expect our spouses to be able to read our minds. Even when we don't make ourselves clear, we imagine that they know what we mean. It is as if we expected our spouses to become clairvoyant after we were married.

This isn't always fair to our spouses. In fact, many times we don't even know what we mean ourselves, so how can we assume that our spouses will understand what we are trying to say? Don't expect your spouse to be a mind reader and know what you mean if you don't even know yourself.

42. "I DIDN'T THINK YOU WOULD MIND IF I TOLD PEOPLE ABOUT YOUR _____"

There are certain things you know about your spouse that you should never tell other people. Violating this trust can have serious consequences. One thing to remember is that your spouse also knows those things that you are most sensitive about and would least want others to know.

You need to be discreet when deciding what things about your partner you will share with other people. Think about how your spouse would react if others knew what you are about to tell them. If there is any question about disclosing some confidence about your loved one, find something else to talk about.

43. "WHAT ARE YOU THINKING ABOUT?"

There is nothing more private than our thoughts. Few people would even think of asking you about your innermost thoughts, except maybe your spouse. Now this is not to say or suggest that we shouldn't use openness and honesty with our spouses. These are the things that successful marriages need to be built upon. It is just that there are some things that we sometimes would rather keep to ourselves.

Don't put your spouse on the spot all the time about what he or she may be thinking. You know the kind of thoughts your partner likes to share as well as the kind he or she would prefer not to reveal. Let your spouse keep some private thoughts private.

44. "I KNOW HOW MUCH YOU HATE TO HEAR THIS."

If you already know how much your spouse hates to hear something, then why are you going to say it anyway? Truthfully, it is probably because you know that your spouse doesn't want to hear it. Why do married people constantly do this to one another? Is it because we do know how much the other hates to hear it?

You may have many good reasons of your own for saying things to your spouse that you know he or she doesn't want to hear. Maybe you are trying to convince your mate of something that he or she refuses to accept. If so, is continuing to bug your spouse about whatever it is he or she doesn't want to hear really doing any good? Is your spouse any closer to changing his or her mind? If the answer is "no," then maybe it's time to stop saying anything about it to your spouse. You are likely just causing more conflict than anything else without making any progress.

45. "YEAH, I'M LISTENING."

"What did you say, again?"

"That's nice."

"Whatever you want, dear."

"Yeah, I'm listening."

All of these statements mean basically the same thing: you are not really listening to your spouse. There is nothing more irritating than trying to talk to someone who is not really listening to you. Instead of admitting to being distracted, your spouse says things like this to create the illusion that he or she is still paying attention and is interested in what you have to say.

Give your spouse your undivided attention when he or she is talking to you. Don't try the old fake-out with these false responses just to make it seem like you are listening. You might just be missing out on something you really do want to hear.

46. "I'M NOT LISTENING TO YOU ANYMORE."

This is simply a more honest way of saying, "Yeah, I'm listening." There are many ways of telling your spouse you are not listening other than simply using these words. You could stick your fingers in your ears. Or you could pretend to be listening and simply nod as if you were paying attention. Regardless, sometimes when we get upset or frustrated with what our spouses have to say, we stop listening and even tell them so.

Listening can be one of the hardest things to do in a marriage. It is also one of the most important. Don't turn your listening on and off in your communications with your spouse. You can't communicate effectively in your marriage if you stop listening to each other.

47. "I DIDN'T KNOW YOU WANTED ME TO CALL."

How should you know that your spouse expected you to call? You have no idea when your partner wants you to call while you are out, or do you?

You surely have some idea when your spouse expects you to call and check in to let him or her know what you are doing or that you are all right if you are running late. Don't make your partner worry about you unnecessarily. Take a moment to phone in when you know your spouse expects a call from you.

48. "I THOUGHT I TOLD YOU I WAS GOING TO BE LATE."

In other words, you got so busy or involved in what you were doing that you didn't bother worrying about getting back in time. Does this more accurately describe why you didn't call or arrive on time than this flimsy excuse?

However, saying this to your spouse may be the only defense you have to explain why you were late. Once you have gotten yourself in this situation, there is really no graceful way out—that is, except for telling him or her the truth about why you are late. It might be easier just to be on time from now on rather than to be making up excuses why you were late.

CHAPTER FIVE

Schedules

101 Things You Should Never Say to Your Spouse

49. "I DON'T HAVE TIME TO TALK ABOUT IT."

Your spouse may have something very important that he or she wants to talk to you about. Saying that you don't have time to talk about it will most likely make this situation even more urgent. You will probably end up spending more time debating why you don't have enough time to listen than it would have taken to listen to what your spouse wanted to tell you in the first place. Find the time to talk to your spouse, especially when it is important to him or her. It will ultimately save you both time and frustration.

50. "I'LL SEND YOU AN E-MAIL INSTEAD OF CALLING."

In our hectic, fast-paced electronic world you may not always have time to telephone your spouse during your busy day. Instead, you could save time by sending your partner an e-mail message. Maybe your spouse won't mind communicating with you electronically rather than over the phone. Or would he or she?

Perhaps this depends on the message, but your spouse would probably rather talk to you "live" over the telephone. Take the time to give him or her a call instead of sending that e-mail.

51. "I'M TOO BUSY TO MEET YOU FOR LUNCH."

Meeting for lunch can be a nice chance for couples to catch up with one another during their busy day. You can get more in touch with what each other is experiencing during the day and gain insight into how your spouse may feel when you see each other again at home later on. All these good things will happen, unless of course you tell your spouse, "I'm too busy to meet you for lunch."

52. "I CAN NEVER SEEM TO REMEMBER WHEN WE ARE SUPPOSED TO DO THINGS TOGETHER."

This is even a bigger problem for your spouse if you have a selective memory for the things you are supposed to do together. In other words, if you seem to have no trouble remembering things that you are to do by yourself in great detail and for long periods of time, you have proven that you can remember dates. Your spouse might just get the feeling that you don't really want to do these things together.

To avoid this misunderstanding, you might want to share an appointment calendar to keep track of these upcoming events that you will be sharing.

53. "I CHANGED OUR PLANS."

In truth the statement, "I changed our plans" should rightfully be followed by, "without consulting with you first." If these changes in plans are not well received by your spouse, don't be surprised. Very few people appreciate having their plans changed without first being asked if they mind or not. How do you know that these changes are not causing some other conflict for your spouse?

Think about how you would feel if your plans were changed without your being told. Let your spouse know before you change plans rather than afterwards. You will be amazed how much more supportive he or she may be about making new plans in the future when consulted beforehand.

101 Things You Should Never Say to Your Spouse

CHAPTER SIX

Time Off

101 Things You Should Never Say to Your Spouse

54. "YOU'VE GOT TO READ THIS BOOK."

Just because your spouse married you doesn't mean that he or she has to share your taste in entertainment. No matter how much you may have enjoyed the book you just finished reading, it is possible that your spouse will not. Don't insist that your partner read everything that interests you. Are you always interested in reading the books your spouse enjoys? If the answer is "no," then you and your spouse definitely have different reading preferences and tastes. Honor these differences.

55. "I NEED MORE TIME TO MYSELF."

We all need to have some time to ourselves. People are so busy with the responsibilities of work, home, and family today that often there is little or no time left to do what they really want to do. Finding time to pursue your own interests or just to relax is great, as long as it doesn't create problems for your spouse.

The success you might have in asking your spouse for more time to do what you want to do may depend more on timing than on anything else. You need to pick those times when your partner doesn't have other plans for the two of you together. You could also help your spouse plan for some solitary time of his or her own.

56. "I'LL DECIDE WHERE WE GO ON VACATION."

Deciding where the two of you will go on your vacation can be half the fun of the entire experience. At least it will be for you, if you make all the decisions concerning where you will vacation each year. Ask your spouse if he or she is really happy with your choice of vacation spots every year. If you get an answer that is less than an enthusiastic "yes," then maybe it's time that you sat down together with some travel brochures to discuss your next vacation destination.

57. "I DON'T WANT TO DO ANYTHING NEW OR DIFFERENT TOGETHER."

Are you tired of doing the same old things together as a couple? Well, even if you aren't, maybe your spouse is. You need to keep an open mind about doing new and different things with your spouse.

Like an old television commercial used to say, "Try it, you'll like it"! Don't immediately reject any suggestion your spouse presents about doing something different. You never know, you might just like it.

58. "GIVE ME THE TV CLICKER."

Before cable television and remote controls became household essentials, the issue of deciding which channel to watch wasn't a big deal for couples. Now as a result of all the new entertainment technology, a whole new power struggle has emerged for today's couples: the fight to control the TV clicker!

Surfing through all 275 channels offered by your local cable company just isn't the same if your spouse is controlling the clicker. It is a bit like having your spouse turn you into a schizophrenic. Just when you are getting interested in a program that suddenly appeared on the screen, click! goes the remote, and you are watching something else.

You need to come to some kind of arrangement about who has control of the clicker in your home. Perhaps a joint custody agreement for the remote control might work.

59. "I DON'T FEEL LIKE GOING AWAY TOGETHER THIS WEEKEND."

This statement will surely take away some of the romance for your spouse concerning your plans for getting away together this weekend. Just because you have decided that you are not going to enjoy yourself this weekend, why do you have to spoil it for your loved one?

This is what is called a self-fulfilling prophecy. Something happens precisely because you have decided it will happen. It's like saying, "I'm not going to enjoy myself at the party." If you go to a party with this negative mindset, you won't enjoy yourself. So change your attitude about going away together, pack your bag for the weekend, and get in a more romantic mood.

60. "LET'S EAT AT HOME AGAIN TONIGHT."

The old saying, "There is nothing like home cooking," is really only true if you are not the one doing the cooking. If this is the case in your home, maybe your spouse would like to take a break from cooking and go out to eat once in a while.

Don't insist on eating at home all the time. You and your spouse need to go out to a restaurant on occasion to relax and enjoy a meal together. The really great thing about going out to eat is that you don't have to do the dishes afterward.

61. "LET'S NOT DO ANYTHING SPECIAL THIS HOLIDAY."

Why don't you decide right now what your spouse will do every holiday from here to eternity? Maybe you already have? If you never want to do anything different or special on holidays, that is exactly what you have already done.

If this has been your attitude, you need to listen to what your spouse might like to do to celebrate your next holiday together. Sometimes new traditions are just as good as old ones, maybe even better.

62. "LET ME READ THE SUNDAY PAPER FIRST."

Don't you just hate trying to read the Sunday paper after someone else has completely dismantled it, section by section? There is no longer any flow or continuity to the paper, not to mention that it looks like it was caught in a windstorm. Do you secretly try to get up earlier than your spouse on Sunday mornings just to get to read the paper first? Do you leave the paper in a mess, forcing your spouse to try to put the pages back together into some kind of coherent order to read it?

If you answered "yes" to any of the above questions, then maybe it is time for you to give your spouse first read of the Sunday paper. Let him or her enjoy the pleasure of having each of the paper's sections neatly folded and in the correct order with all the inserts intact. It might be interesting to see what condition the newspaper is in when it's your turn to read it.

63. "GIVE ME A BACK MASSAGE."

After you have been married for a while, back massages tend to become much less frequent. They also become much more fun to receive than to give. This is particularly true if you have no intention of reciprocating the massage to your spouse. Back massages can become tough, physical work for your spouse with little or no reward under these circumstances.

Don't obligate your spouse to give you back massages without some expectation of reciprocation. This could include many different things, such as expressing your gratitude or even returning the favor. Remember the "back" in back massages and give one "back" to your spouse.

64. "DO WE HAVE TO GO OUT WITH THEM?"

Implied by this question is that your spouse is looking forward to going out with the other couple and you are not. This can present quite a dilemma for you both. How do you keep peace in the family and at the same time not insult your friends?

The best solution to this problem is for you to change your attitude about going out with the other couple. The way you're presently headed will only cause unpleasantness for everyone involved. Keep your feelings about going out with these people to yourself and just try to have a good time. You might even end up enjoying their company after all.

65. "JUST READ MY MAGAZINES INSTEAD OF SUBSCRIBING TO YOUR OWN."

Nowadays there seems to be a magazine designed to suit just about anyone's special interests. It is very likely that those magazines that are interesting to you might not be of interest to your spouse. You may no more care for auto racing than your spouse does for needlepoint or vice versa.

Then why would you even suggest that your spouse would be happy reading your magazines? If necessary, give up one of your magazine subscriptions to allow your partner to subscribe to something he or she would be interested in reading. Your loved one will appreciate you a little bit more every time his or her magazine arrives in the mail.

66. "I'LL CHOOSE THE MOVIE WE SEE TONIGHT."

With the multiple-screen theaters available today, deciding which movie you and your spouse will see can be a difficult process. Typically, it comes down to a choice between two films: the one you want to see and the one your spouse wants to see. Which one do you go to see? The choice should be obvious!

Actually, you and your spouse should take turns choosing the movies you will see when you go out to a theater. Wasn't that your solution?

101 Things You Should Never Say to Your Spouse

CHAPTER SEVEN

Roles

101 Things You Should Never Say to Your Spouse

67. "YOU DO ALL THE COOKING."

Is your spouse the short-order cook in your home? Why don't you just ask for a menu so you can tell him or her exactly what you want for dinner this evening? In addition to all the cooking, do you also make your spouse do all the grocery shopping and wash the dishes after the meal? If so, you should be leaving a tip at the end of every meal you eat at home.

If this describes how the meals are prepared and served in your home, maybe it is time for a change. Ask your spouse how you can help with the cooking and share in these responsibilities. You may really get "cooking" together!

68. "YOU MAKE THE COFFEE IN THE MORNING."

Why don't you just put it to your spouse this way: "Congratulations, I'm naming you the full-time, permanent morning-coffee maker in our home." Don't you think any husband or wife would feel honored to receive this very prestigious distinction?

Of course that question doesn't even deserve an answer. Don't designate your spouse the official Coffee Maker in the family. Share the morning coffee-making responsibilities if you do not already. Surprise your spouse tomorrow morning with a fresh pot of coffee when he or she wakes up. Even better, bring a cup to your spouse before he or she gets out of bed.

69. "I'M SICK OF HEARING ABOUT YOUR WORK."

Your spouse is supposed to be the one person in this world who will listen sympathetically to the continuing saga of all your problems at work. Hearing that your partner is no longer willing to let you share these career frustrations can be devastating. Who will be there to listen to your spouse talking about what a so-and-so the boss is or how he or she was unjustifiably passed over for that big promotion?

Don't underestimate how important it is to your spouse for you to lend a sympathetic ear while he or she discusses problems at work.

70. "DON'T WORRY ABOUT YOUR JOB SO MUCH."

This might be one of those things in life that are easier said than done. It may be simple for you to minimize your spouse's problems at work, but then you're not the one who has to face them each day. Instead of telling your spouse not to worry about work problems so much, help him or her find possible solutions to them. Even if you can't resolve the difficulties, just being able to talk about these problems with you may help your spouse to deal with them more effectively.

71. "TAKE OUT THE GARBAGE."

Telling your spouse to throw out the trash is like saying, "You do all the dirty work around here." Is that really any way to treat the one you love?

Take your turn doing those unpleasant tasks around your home and don't stick your partner with all the jobs you don't want to do. Surprise your spouse. Take the garbage out today and complete some other chores you don't normally do without being asked or complaining about having to do them.

101 Things You Should Never Say to Your Spouse

CHAPTER EIGHT

Compatibility

101 Things You Should Never Say to Your Spouse

72. "I'M NOT GOING TO FIGHT FAIR."

All is fair in love and war, or so they say. So why should you agree to fight fair? Well, for one thing, you also will want to make up afterwards. You don't want to win the battle only to lose the war. During fights, spouses often say things they don't really mean. Be careful about what you say to your spouse even during an argument. Remember that you love this person you are fighting with!

During a marital squabble, don't say things that you would never dare to say to any other person in this world or to your spouse at any other time. Otherwise, on one of these occasions your partner may not be as forgiving after the argument is over. Fight fairly and maturely. Express why you are upset, but don't say things just to hurt your spouse. They will ultimately hurt you as well.

73. "I WON'T LET IT GO."

Holding grudges against your spouse can be very self-destructive. Carrying this resentment around with you may eventually weigh you down to the point that it completely overpowers you. Unburden yourself and your spouse from these grudges. You both will feel a lot lighter as a result.

74. "I DON'T FEEL LIKE TAKING A WALK TOGETHER."

Taking a walk together is an excellent way to spend some time alone with your spouse away from everything and everyone else. It gives you a chance to get caught up on what is going on in each other's lives while you are apart each day. It's also great exercise.

Realizing all of these positive consequences, why would you object to going for a walk with your spouse? Put on a pair of comfortable shoes and get walking!

75. "YOU ARE SO PREDICTABLE."

Habits. We all have them. It doesn't take our spouses very long to learn and anticipate our routines. Our partners know how we will react in different situations and what we will say about things before we utter a word. Our spouses become the experts on us.

However, most people do not like to be thought of as being predictable. They want to have some mystery about themselves and still be able to surprise their spouses from time to time. Even if you could perfectly predict just about everything your spouse will do, maybe it is not such a good idea to let him or her know. In the future, you just may find this skill at predicting your spouse's behavior to be more useful if he or she isn't aware of it.

76. "YOU'RE ALWAYS IN A BAD MOOD."

If your spouse is already in a bad mood, saying this to him or her will only serve to make matters worse. You know what usually puts your partner in a foul humor. Try to do whatever you can to avoid these things or at least help your loved one to deal with them better. Or you can continue to make your spouse's frame of mind even worse, but remember that you are the one who will be the recipient of these bad moods. Find something to say to your partner that has a better chance of improving his or her mood. "I love you" or "Can I do something to help you?" might work pretty well for starters.

77. "WHAT'S BUGGING YOU?"

There are certainly more diplomatic ways of asking this question. Other options might be, "You seem out of sorts today. Is there anything bothering you?" Or you might say, "Is there something I did that is upsetting you?"

Or you could continue to make your spouse even more upset than he or she already is. The real question is this: Are you really interested in knowing what might be upsetting your mate or are you just angry that he or she is behaving this way? The answer to this question will determine how successful you are in finding out what is really bothering your spouse.

78. "IS THAT SMELL YOU?"

There may be any number of reasons why your spouse may smell different to you. He or she may be wearing a new cologne or perfume. Or your mate may have just switched to a new brand of deodorant or shampoo that has a different scent than the old one. There could also be other, less pleasant reasons for your spouse to smell different.

Before just blurting out, "What is that smell?" when coming into close contact with your spouse, you need to consider a few other options. You may ask if there was a sale on soap or other personal hygiene items at the store. Or, if you are really diplomatic and romantic, you could suggest that the two of you take a shower together!

79. "YOU SHOULD HAVE KNOWN THAT I NEEDED HELP."

Do you expect your spouse to always know when you need help? Did you tell him or her that you needed help? If not, why do you assume that your partner knows?

Often we expect our spouses to know when we need a helping hand without ever asking for it. Maybe we are more interested in griping about not getting assistance than in actually getting it from our spouses. Stop playing games and let your mate know when you need help. Otherwise, don't complain when you have to handle things yourself.

80. "YOU'LL NEVER CHANGE MY MIND."

Now there is a challenge. The more you stand your ground on something you disagree about with your spouse, the more determined he or she might become to change your mind. Actually saying, "You'll never change my mind about this" is like waving a red flag in front of a bull.

  A better strategy would be to keep an open mind about at least discussing the issue. Declaring your inflexibility may only serve to shut down any communications there could be on the subject. You can still make any decision you want after listening to how your partner feels. At least this way you will know more about why your spouse feels this way and he or she can better understand your position.

101 Things You Should Never Say to Your Spouse

CHAPTER NINE

Lifestyles

101 Things You Should Never Say to Your Spouse

81. "WHY SHOULD WE WORRY ABOUT RETIREMENT PLANNING NOW?"

Hopefully in every marriage there is at least one partner who is interested in retirement planning. Otherwise nothing may ever be put aside to make your retirement together more comfortable and enjoyable. If both of you have a "why worry?" attitude about retirement planning, at least one of you needs to change your thinking about the future.

Begin planning for your retirement together. It will be here sooner than you think.

82. "I WAS GOING TO BUY IT FOR YOU BUT IT WAS TOO EXPENSIVE."

There are at least two major problems with saying this to your spouse. First, you have just told your partner that money is more important than making him or her happy. The second drawback is that your spouse probably would have been happier if you had never said anything about the purchase that never happened.

You should either buy the item for your spouse or say nothing about it at all. Don't tease your partner by telling him or her how close you came to purchasing that expensive gift.

83. "WHY DID YOU THROW THAT OUT?"

In every marriage there is a "thrower" and a "saver." There always seems to be one of each in every relationship. Throwers throw away everything and savers save everything. This is called balance in marriage. It protects couples from disposing of all their possessions the instant they think they are no longer necessary. It also prevents couples from holding onto everything they have ever acquired until they need a warehouse to store it all. If both partners are either throwers or savers when they get married, one of them will begin to adopt the opposite tendency.

This principle is very important to maintaining balance in a marriage. It can also be a source of frustration to each partner in the relationship. The saver gets upset when a spouse throws things out, and the thrower doesn't like it when things accumulate in the home. If you are constantly complaining that your spouse is wrongly throwing something out, you are probably a saver. If you complain that your spouse never discards anything, you are probably a thrower. Complaining will do you no good. You are fighting the forces of nature as well as disturbing the delicate balance of throwers and savers in a marriage.

84. "WHAT'S FOR BREAKFAST?"

This question's built-in implication is that you expect your spouse to make breakfast for you this morning. Another way to ask this question might be, "What would you like me to make for breakfast this morning?" To which phrasing do you think your spouse would be more receptive?

There are few better ways to start a day than to find that someone has breakfast ready for you when you get up in the morning. Why not share this enjoyment with each other? Take turns getting up earlier and preparing breakfast for one another, particularly on special occasions and at milestones in your life together.

85. "STOP PUTTING IT OFF AND JUST DO IT."

Spouses have been saying, "Just do it" since long before the commercials and advertisements made this phrase so popular. The difference is that spouses have been trying to get their mates to do the things they hate to do rather than to pursue an athletic dream or passion.

If you keep pestering your spouse to do something, he or she may become even more resistant to doing it. If you stop reminding him or her, you will undoubtedly hear something like, "Why didn't you remind me to do that?"

You most likely can't win under any circumstances when trying to get your spouse to do something he or she doesn't want to do. Go ahead and try, but be prepared for less than favorable results!

86. "I FORGOT TO TELL YOU WHAT I BOUGHT."

Now this confession would not be a problem if it were followed by, "It's a present for you." If that is the case, you have absolutely nothing to worry about. However, anything else may require a bit more explanation. Most couples have to watch their spending, and sometimes one purchase may make a big difference in their budgets. The purchase you make without your spouse's knowledge may put an end to the purchase of something that he or she really wanted to buy. Maybe before you make your next purchase you should discuss it with your spouse.

87. "I DIDN'T KNOW YOU WANTED TO GO."

It's not that you didn't want your spouse to go with you or anything like that. Of course you wanted your spouse to join you. It was just that you never dreamed that he or she would be interested in coming with you.

On the other hand, perhaps you did not merely forget to invite your spouse to come? Suppose that realizing this to be the case, your spouse confronts you with the evidence that he or she has gathered to prove that you really didn't want the company. What would you say? Most likely it would be something like, "I didn't know you wanted to go." Maybe you should just save yourselves all this time and frustration and invite your spouse to come along.

101 Things You Should Never Say to Your Spouse

CHAPTER TEN

Romance

101 Things You Should Never Say to Your Spouse

88. "WHO CARES ABOUT REMINISCING ABOUT WHEN WE FIRST MET?"

The time of their lives when couples first meet is very special. Your spouse may cherish these memories and enjoy talking about those early romantic days of your relationship. Denying your loved one this opportunity will probably not be very much appreciated. Enjoy reminiscing with your spouse about those days and rekindle some of the romance of the times when you first fell in love. Be receptive to revisiting your shared past. Like history lessons in school, these stories from back then can help you better understand your relationship today.

89. "WE'RE MARRIED, SO WE CAN'T GO ON DATES ANYMORE."

You may believe that married people don't go on dates together anymore. However, your spouse may not agree. Being married doesn't mean you can't go out and enjoy each other's company. Make a date with your spouse for next weekend. Do some of the same things you did together before you were married. You might be surprised by how much it feels like the times when you were just dating.

90. "IT'S STUPID TO CELEBRATE OUR ANNIVERSARY."

You might as well say to your spouse, "I don't like to remember unpleasant experiences I have had in my life"! Celebrating your wedding anniversary is an opportunity to remember how you felt about each other on your wedding day. Your anniversary is a chance to get back in touch with those old feelings and to put your relationship today into perspective. Celebrate your life together rather than letting this opportunity to renew your feelings for one another pass you by.

91. "DON'T CALL ME THAT ANYMORE."

Spouses often have pet names for each other. These are actually special ways that they express their love for one another. As time passes by, sometimes these special names begin to sound kind of silly. Don't let that happen to you and your loved one. Cherish the special name that your spouse has for you and accept it as a constant expression of his or her love every time you hear it.

92. "I DIDN'T HAVE TIME TO GET YOU A CARD."

It is not as if there weren't any number of stores that specialize in selling cards for just about any occasion. You would almost have to go out of your way not to pass by some place that sells greeting cards on a daily basis. Then why is it so difficult for you to find the time to get your spouse a card for a special occasion?

If you were honest with both yourself and your spouse, you would admit that it really wasn't lack of time as much as selfishness, insensitivity, taking your spouse for granted, and even poor planning that prevented you from getting that special card. Use the "ran out of time" excuse to save face for not getting your spouse a card one last time. Then make a commitment to find the time to get a card for your spouse on every special occasion in the future.

93. "I DON'T NEED TO SAY 'THANK YOU' TO YOU."

Do you think that once you are married you are still required to use common courtesies with your spouse? Are expressions such as "Please," "Thank you," "Would you mind," or "That was very nice of you" really still necessary when talking with your spouse? Why should you treat the person that you love with less courtesy than you would extend to other people, some of whom you might not even like? It just makes sense that you should treat your spouse with the same, if not more, consideration than you would other people.

94. "I'M NOT GOING TO WEAR MY WEDDING RING ANYMORE."

There are few reasons for not wearing your wedding ring that will be acceptable to your spouse. One might be that you had to leave it at the jewelers to get it repaired. However, if these repairs take weeks, months, or even years to complete, your spouse may begin to doubt your interest in wearing your wedding ring anymore.

Your wedding ring is more than just a way of telling the world that you are married. Your ring is a symbol of your love and commitment to your spouse. Keep it on.

95. "WHY DO YOU WANT TO HOLD HANDS?"

Do you think that holding hands in public after being married all these years is stupid? Does it seem that holding hands is for kids and not for grown-up married people? Well, maybe you should look around next time you are out together. There are a lot of grown-up married people out there acting like kids again. Maybe you should join them.

What would it hurt to behave as you did when you first met and were dating? You are still the same people, and you both have the capacity now to feel just the way you did about each other back then. Hold hands again. It can bring you closer to one another and more in touch!

96. "I DON'T LIKE TO KISS ANYMORE."

Like holding hands, kissing may be another one of those things that you believe married people don't do anymore. This list of activities that matrimony supposedly puts an end to can go on and on! Kissing is not just a prelude to marriage but also an expression of the love you have for one another for all of your life together.

Don't stop kissing. Just as it was in the beginning of your relationship, kissing is important as a way of sharing the intimacy you feel towards each other. You are never too old to do a little necking.

97. "I FORGOT TO BUY YOU A PRESENT."

There is nothing that you can say after this announcement that will get you out of trouble. Even if you go out and get your spouse a belated present, it still won't be the same. You will be better off than you would be if you didn't buy him or her a gift at all, but don't kid yourself. You will still be in very hot water.

Avoid getting yourself in this predicament over and over again. Buy something you know your spouse will like, wrap it, and hide it away. This way you will be ready for any occasion that may come up when you are expected to have a gift for your spouse.

98. "SURE, I MISSED YOU WHEN YOU WERE GONE."

If you find yourself saying this, you are no doubt responding to your spouse's question as to whether or not you missed him or her. If this is the case, you have let things get out of control. You need to tell your spouse how much you missed him or her while you were apart before the question is asked. Your spouse will be much more likely to believe you really missed him or her if that sentiment does not have to be aggressively wrenched out of you. Don't turn a potential positive into a negative.

99. "I DON'T WANT TO TALK ABOUT US."

Sometimes one partner in a marriage is reluctant to discuss their relationship. This makes it difficult to even begin to address marital problems they may be experiencing. Each spouse needs to be ready to share intimate thoughts and feelings about their relationship and life together.

You need to be willing to not only discuss your relationship with your spouse but also explore ways that it can be improved. All this begins by talking about this with your spouse. Keep these important lines of communication open.

100. "I DON'T HAVE TO WORRY ABOUT MY APPEARANCE ANYMORE—YOU'LL LOVE ME ANYWAY."

This may indeed be true, but it may not do much for your relationship. Letting your appearance go just because you are married may not prove to be a good long-term plan for your marriage or even possibly your health.

Although there is certainly much more to a relationship besides physical appearance, it is still important to look attractive to your spouse. This can help to keep your spouse interested in you as well as improve your own self-image and confidence. All of these things are important in a marriage.

101. "I DON'T FEEL LIKE MAKING LOVE."

This last one requires no explanation. This is something that you and your spouse need to resolve together. All of the preceding 100 things you shouldn't say might just be forgiven if you can work this one out!

About the Authors

Peter R. Garber
and
Nancy C. Garber

Peter and Nancy Garber have been married for over thirty years and believe that they have said nearly all of these *101 Things You Should Never Say to Your Spouse* to one another. Peter and Nancy met while both students at the University of Pittsburgh where they attended creative writing classes together. Peter began his career as a Human

Resource Professional in 1980 which lead to the family moving across the country a number of times as his career progressed. They have two daughters, Lauren born in 1982 and Erin born in 1986, both now in college. Nancy stayed home with the children until their High School years when she became a Flight Attendant with major airline. As in any marriage, every change brings new challenges and stresses resulting in many things being said. Regardless of what they say to one another, Peter and Nancy always find a way to make sure that there is love in every message.

Peter has written over 40 books and articles on a variety of business life topics including his highly acclaimed *Turbulent Change: Every Working Person's Survival Guide*; *Giving and Receiving Performance Feedback*; *99 Ways to Keep Employees Happy, Satisfied, Motivated and Productive* and *101 Stupid Things Supervisors Do To Sabotage Success*. He has also recently released two new books: *Winning the Rat Race at Work* and *100 Ways to Get on the Wrong Side of Your Boss*, both published by Multi-Media Publications. With Nancy's encouragement and help, *101 Things You Should Never Say to Your Spouse* is his first book about personal relationships.

Want to Get Ahead in Your Career?

Do you find yourself challenged by office politics, bad things happen-ing to good careers, dealing with the "big cheeses" at work, the need for effective networking skills, and keeping good working relation-ships with coworkers and bosses? *Winning the Rat Race at Work* is a unique book that provides you with case studies, interactive exercises, self-assessments, strategies, evaluations, and models for overcoming these workplace challenges. The book illustrates the stages of a career and the career choices that determine your future, empowering you to make positive changes.

Written by Peter R. Garber, the author of *100 Ways to Get on the Wrong Side of Your Boss*, this book is a must read for anyone interested in getting ahead in his or her career. You will want to keep a copy in your top desk drawer for ready reference whenever you find yourself in a challenging predicament at work.

ISBN: 1-895186-68-4 (paperback)
Also available in ebook formats. Order from your local bookseller, Amazon.com, or directly from the publisher at **http://www.mmpubs.com/rats**

Need More Help with the Politics at Work?

100 Ways To Get On The Wrong Side Of Your Boss (And Strategies to Prevent You from Getting There!) was written for anyone who has ever been frustrated by his or her working relationship with the boss—and who hasn't ever felt this way! Bosses play a critically important role in your career success and getting on the wrong side of this important individual in your working life is not a good thing.

Each of these 100 Ways is designed to illustrate a particular problem that you may encounter when dealing with your boss and then an effective strategy to prevent this problem from reoccurring. You will learn how to deal more effectively with your boss in this fun and practical book filled with invaluable advice that can be utilized every day at work.

Written by Peter R. Garber, the author of *Winning the Rat Race at Work*, this book is a must read for anyone interested in getting ahead. You will want to keep a copy in your top desk drawer for ready reference whenever you find yourself in a challenging predicament at work.

ISBN: 1-895186-98-6   (paperback)
Also available in ebook formats. Order from your local bookseller, Amazon.com, or directly from the publisher at **http://www.InTroubleAtWork.com**

Changing Jobs? Get Started on the Right Foot

Studies show that your working relationship with the boss is one of the top factors in job satisfaction. Whether you have a new job, or a new boss in your current job, you need to focus on building a solid working relationship with this very important person in your work life.

This ebook by human resources guru Peter R. Garber gives you tips on how to forge a positive relationship and get on the good side of your new boss. Start out on the right foot and read this book today!

ISBN: 1-897326-18-1 (Adobe Acrobat PDF)
ISBN: 1-897326-19-X (Microsoft Reader LIT)
ISBN: 1-897326-20-3 (Palm Reader PDB)
ISBN: 1-897326-21-1 (Mobipocket Reader PRC)

Order from all major online ebook retailers, or direct from the publisher at **www.mmpubs.com**

Your wallet is empty? And you still need to boost your team's performance?

Building team morale is difficult in these tough economic times. Author Kevin Aguanno helps you solve the team morale problem with ideas for team rewards that won't break the bank.

Learn over 100 ways you can reward your project team and individual team members for just a few dollars. Full of innovative (and cheap!) ideas. Even with the best reward ideas, rewards can fall flat if they are not suitable to the person, the organization, the situation, or the magnitude of the accomplishment. Learn the four key factors that will *maximize* the impact of your rewards, and *guarantee* delighted recipients.

101 Ways to Reward Team Members for $20 (or Less!) teaches you how to improve employee morale, improve employee motivation, improve departmental and cross-organizational teaming, maximize the benefits of your rewards and recognition programme, and avoid the common mistakes.

ISBN: 1-895186-04-8   (paperback)
Also available in ebook formats. Order from your local bookseller, Amazon.com, or directly from the publisher at **http://www.mmpubs.com**

Corporate Intelligence Awareness: Securing the Competitive Edge

In this compelling new book by a former diplomat, you will learn the secrets (step by step) to developing an intelligence strategy by effective information gathering and analyzing, and then to delivering credible intelligence to senior management. Along the way, you will learn how to better read people and organizations and get them to open up and share information with you—all the while behaving in an ethical, legal manner. Understanding how intelligence is gathered and processed will keep you ahead of the game, protect your secrets, and secure your competitive edge!

ISBN: 1-895186-42-0 (hardcover)
ISBN: 1-895186-43-9 (PDF ebook)

Also available in other ebook formats. Order from your local bookseller, Amazon.com, or directly from the publisher at **http://www.mmpubs.com/cia**

Churchill's Adaptive Enterprise: Lessons for Business Today

This book analyzes a period of time from World War II when Winston Churchill, one of history's most famous leaders, faced near defeat for the British in the face of sustained German attacks. The book describes the strategies he used to overcome incredible odds and turn the tide on the impending invasion. The historical analysis is done through a modern business and information technology lens, describing Churchill's actions and strategy using modern business tools and techniques. Aimed at business executives, IT managers, and project managers, the book extracts learnings from Churchill's experiences that can be applied to business problems today. Particular themes in the book are knowledge management, information portals, adaptive enterprises, and organizational agility.

2007 Eric Hoffer Book Award Winner

ISBN: 1-895186-19-6 (paperback)
ISBN: 1-895186-20-X (PDF ebook)

http://www.mmpubs.com/churchill

Avoiding Project Disaster: Titanic Lessons for IT Executives

Imagine you are in one of *Titanic's* lifeboats. As you look back at the wreckage site, you wonder what could have happened. What were the causes? How could things have gone so badly wrong?

Titanic's maiden voyage was a disaster waiting to happen as a result of the compromises made in the project that constructed the ship. This book explores how modern executives can take lessons from a nuts-and-bolts construction project like *Titanic* and use those lessons to ensure the right approach to developing online business solutions. Looking at this historical project as a model will prove to be incisive as it cuts away the layers of IT jargon and complexity.

Avoiding Project Disaster is about delivering IT projects in a world where being on time and on budget is not enough. You also need to be up and running around the clock for your customers and partners. This book will help you successfully maneuver through the ice floes of IT management in an industry with a notoriously high project failure rate.

ISBN: 1-895186-73-0   (paperback)
Also available in ebook formats.

http://www.mmpubs.com/disaster

Managing Smaller Projects:
A Practical Approach

So called "small projects" can have potentially alarming consequences if they go wrong, but their control is often left to chance. The solution is to adapt tried and tested project management techniques.

This book provides a low overhead, highly practical way of looking after small projects. It covers all the essential skills: from project start-up, to managing risk, quality and change, through to controlling the project with a simple control system. It cuts through the jargon of project management and provides a framework that is as useful to those lacking formal training, as it is to those who are skilled project managers and want to control smaller projects without the burden of bureaucracy.

Read this best-selling book from the U.K., now making its North American debut. *IEE Engineering Management* praises the book, noting that "Simply put, this book is about helping people control smaller projects in a logical and effective way, and making the process run smoothly, and is indeed a success in achieving that goal."

Available in print format. Order from your local bookseller, Amazon.com, or directly from the publisher at
www.mmpubs.com/msp

Managing Agile Projects

Are you being asked to manage a project with unclear requirements, high levels of change, or a team using Extreme Programming or other Agile Methods?

If you are a project manager or team leader who is interested in learning the secrets of successfully controlling and delivering agile projects, then this is the book for you.

From learning how agile projects are different from traditional projects, to detailed guidance on a number of agile management techniques and how to introduce them onto your own projects, this book has the insider secrets from some of the industry experts – the visionaries who developed the agile methodologies in the first place.

ISBN: 1-895186-11-0 (paperback)
ISBN: 1-895186-12-9 (PDF ebook)

http://www.agilesecrets.com

Networking *for* Results
THE POWER OF PERSONAL CONTACT

In partnership with Michael J. Hughes, *The* Networking Guru, Multi-Media Publications Inc. has released a new series of books, ebooks, and audio books designed for business and sales professionals who want to get the most out of their networking events and help their career development.

Networking refers to the concept that each of us has a group or "network" of friends, associates and contacts as part of our on-going human activity that we can use to achieve certain objectives.

The *Networking for Results* series of products shows us how to think about networking strategically, and gives us step-by-step techniques for helping ourselves and those around us achieve our goals. By following these practices, we can greatly improve our personal networking effectiveness.

Visit **www.Networking-for-Results.com** for information on specific products in this series, to read free articles on networking skills, or to sign up for a free networking tips newsletter. Products are available from most book, ebook, and audiobook retailers, or directly from the publisher at **www.mmpubs.com.**

 **The Project Management Audio Library**

In a recent CEO survey, the leaders of today's largest corporations identified project management as the top skillset for tomorrow's leaders. In fact, many organizations place their top performers in project management roles to groom them for senior management positions. Project managers represent some of the busiest people around. They are the ones responsible for planning, executing, and controlling most major new business activities.

Expanding upon the successful *Project Management Essentials Library* series of print and electronic books, Multi-Media Publications has launched a new imprint called the *Project Management Audio Library*. Under this new imprint, MMP is publishing audiobooks and recorded seminars focused on professionals who manage individual projects, portfolios of projects, and strategic programmes. The series covers topics including agile project management, risk management, project closeout, interpersonal skills, and other related project management knowledge areas.

This is not going to be just the "same old stuff" on the critical path method, earned value, and resource levelling; rather, the series will have the latest tips and techniques from those who are at the cutting edge of project management research and real-world application.

www.PM-Audiobooks.com

www.ingramcontent.com/pod-product-compliance
Ingram Content Group UK Ltd.
Pitfield, Milton Keynes, MK11 3LW, UK
UKHW041419180426